FOR ORGANS, PIANOS & ELECTRONIC KEYBOARDS

E-Z PLAY TODAY

20

HYMNS

D0520012

HAL•LEONARD
CORPORATION

7777 W. BLUEMOUND RD. P.O. BOX 13819 MILWAUKEE, WI 53213

E-Z Play © TODAY Music Notation © 1975 HAL LEONARD PUBLISHING CORPORATION
Copyright © 1993 by HAL LEONARD PUBLISHING CORPORATION
International Copyright Secured   All Rights Reserved

E-Z PLAY and EASY ELECTRONIC KEYBOARD MUSIC are registered trademarks of HAL LEONARD PUBLISHING CORPORATION.

ISBN 0-7935 2197-1

All Hail The Power Of Jesus' Name

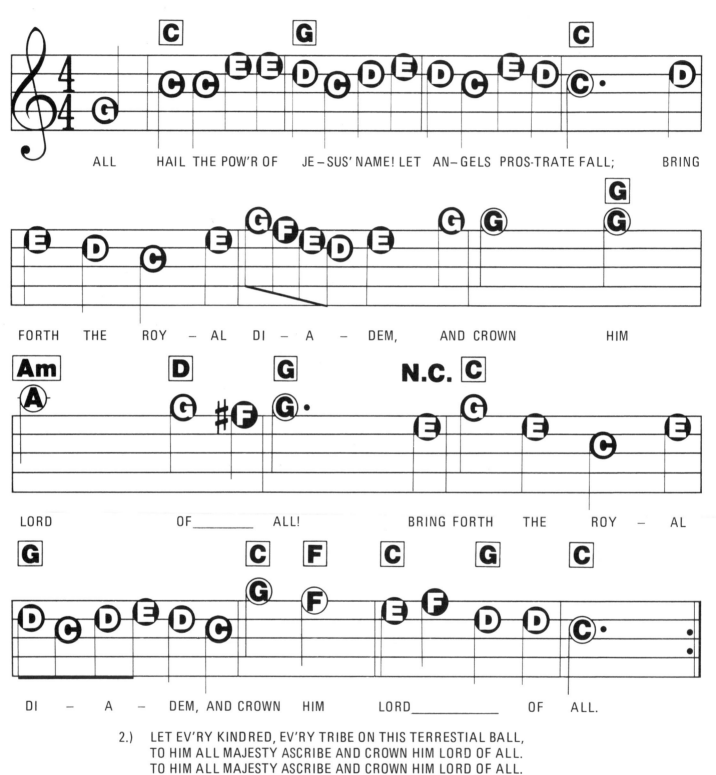

2.) LET EV'RY KINDRED, EV'RY TRIBE ON THIS TERRESTIAL BALL,
TO HIM ALL MAJESTY ASCRIBE AND CROWN HIM LORD OF ALL.
TO HIM ALL MAJESTY ASCRIBE AND CROWN HIM LORD OF ALL.

3.) OH, THAT WITH YONDER SACRED THRONG WE AT HIS FEET MAY FALL.
WE'LL JOIN THE EVERLASTING SONG AND CROWN HIM LORD OF ALL.
WE'LL JOIN THE EVERLASTING SONG AND CROWN HIM LORD OF ALL.

Amazing Grace

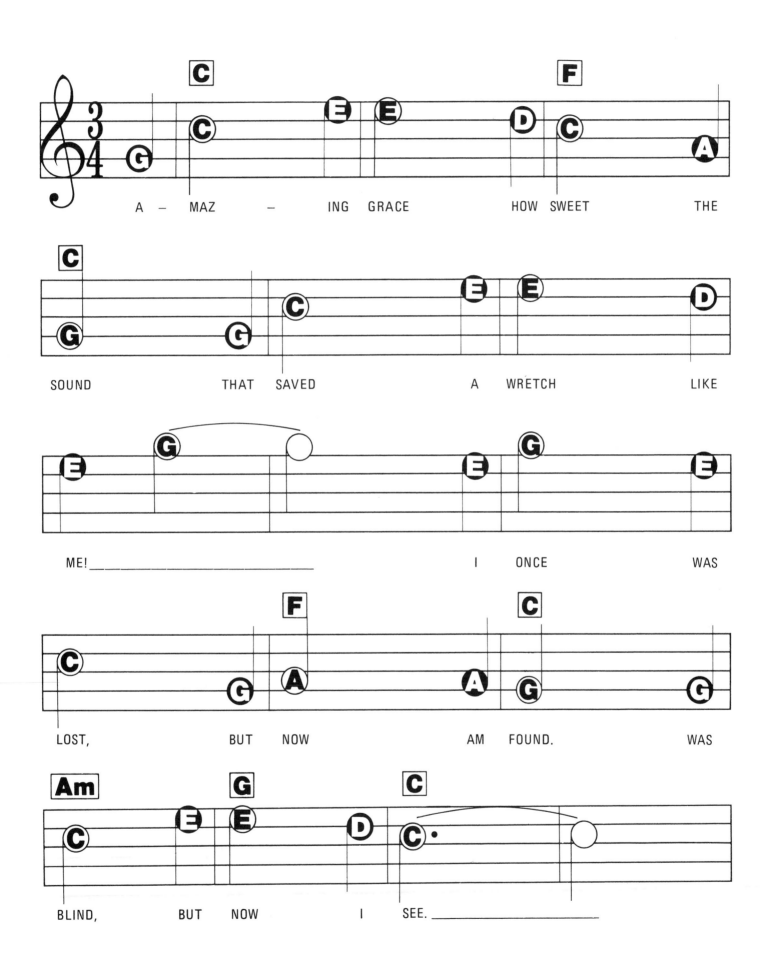

America, The Beautiful

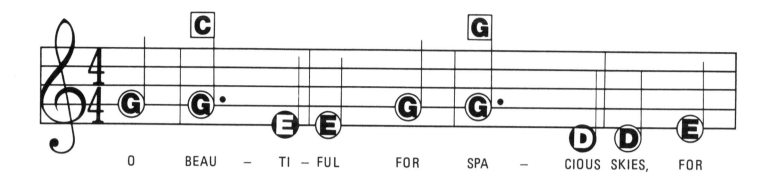

O BEAU – TI – FUL FOR SPA – CIOUS SKIES, FOR

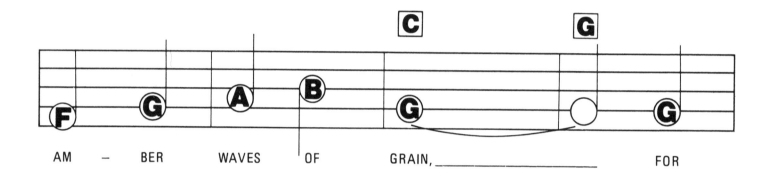

AM – BER WAVES OF GRAIN,_____ FOR

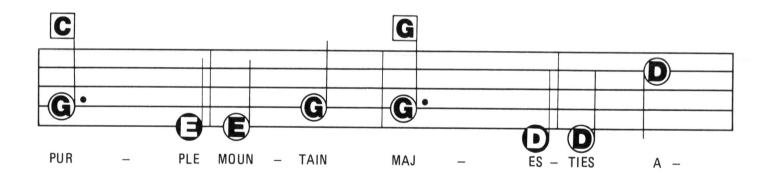

PUR – PLE MOUN – TAIN MAJ – ES – TIES A –

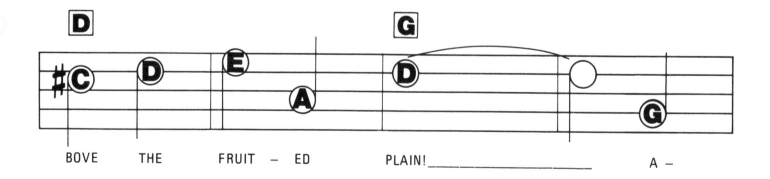

BOVE THE FRUIT – ED PLAIN!_____ A –

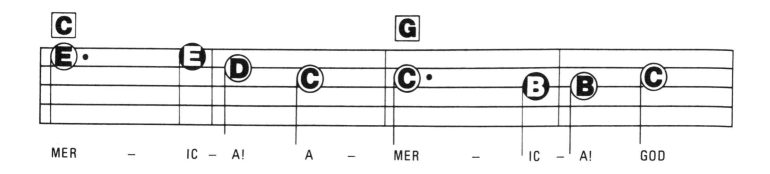

MER — IC — A! A — MER — IC — A! GOD

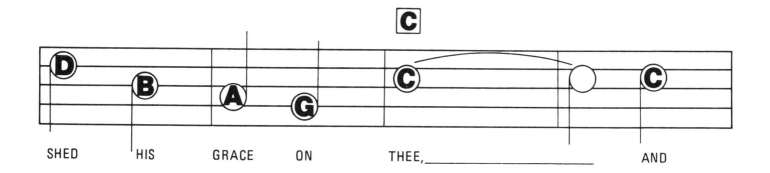

SHED HIS GRACE ON THEE,_____ AND

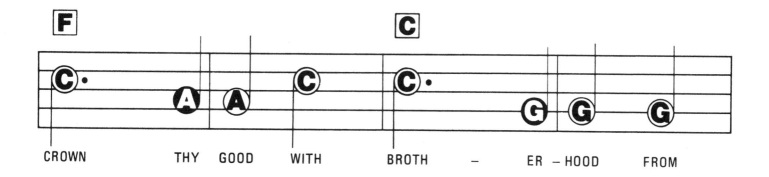

CROWN THY GOOD WITH BROTH — ER — HOOD FROM

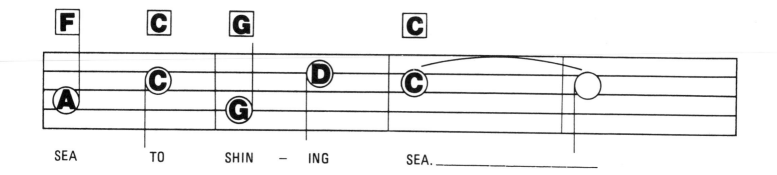

SEA TO SHIN — ING SEA._____

2.) O BEAUTIFUL FOR PILGRIM FEET,
WHOSE STERN, IMPASSIONED STRESS
A THOROUGHFARE FOR FREEDOM BEAT
ACROSS THE WILDERNESS!
AMERICA! AMERICA!
GOD MEND THINE EV'RY FLAW,
CONFIRM THY SOUL IN SELF-CONTROL,
THY LIBERTY IN LAW.

3.) LIFT HIGH THE CROSS, UNFURL THE FLAG;
MAY THEY FOREVER STAND
UNITED IN OUR HEARTS AND HOPES,
GOD AND OUR NATIVE LAND.
AMERICA! AMERICA!
MAY GOD THY LOVE INCREASE,
TILL WARS ARE PAST AND EARTH AT LAST
MAY FOLLOW CHRIST IN PEACE.

Beautiful Isle Of Somewhere

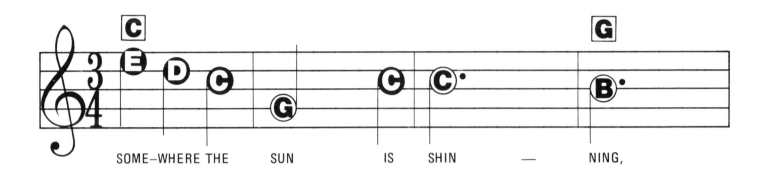

SOME—WHERE THE SUN IS SHIN — NING,

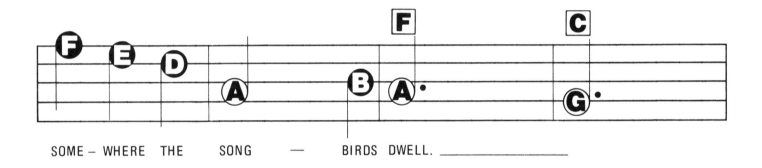

SOME — WHERE THE SONG — BIRDS DWELL. _____

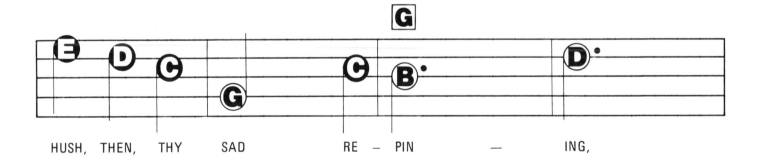

HUSH, THEN, THY SAD RE - PIN — ING,

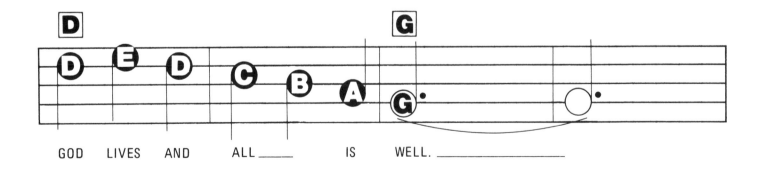

GOD LIVES AND ALL ____ IS WELL. _____

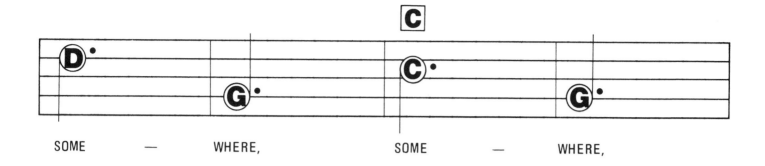

SOME — WHERE, SOME — WHERE,

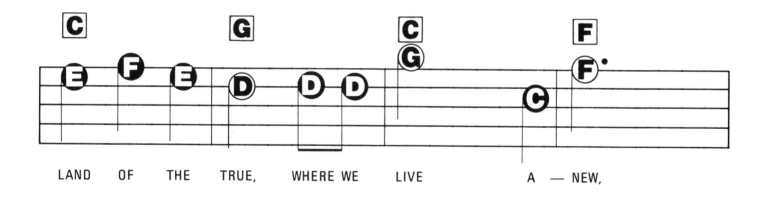

BEAU – TI – FUL ISLE ____ OF SOME — WHERE!

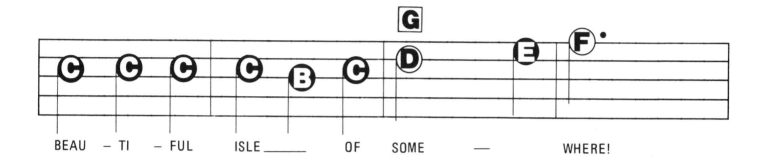

LAND OF THE TRUE, WHERE WE LIVE A — NEW,

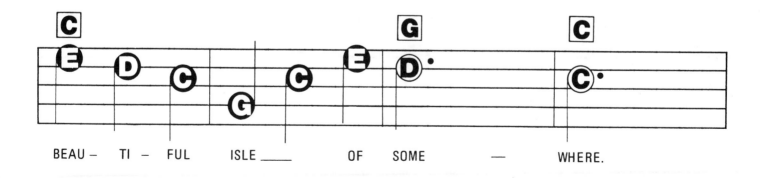

BEAU – TI – FUL ISLE ____ OF SOME — WHERE.

Bringing In The Sheaves

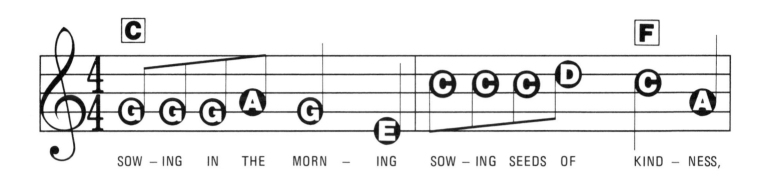

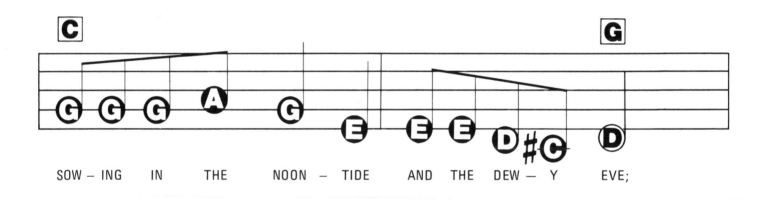

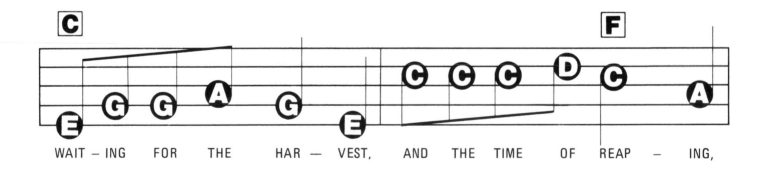

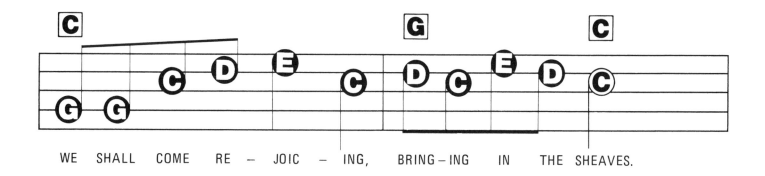

WE SHALL COME RE — JOIC — ING, BRING—ING IN THE SHEAVES.

Chorus

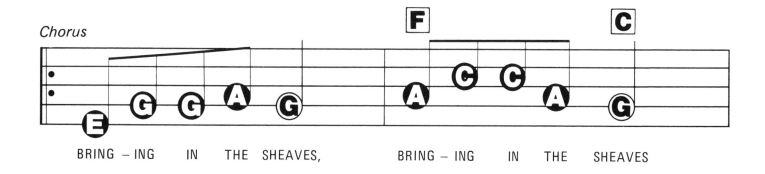

BRING — ING IN THE SHEAVES, BRING — ING IN THE SHEAVES

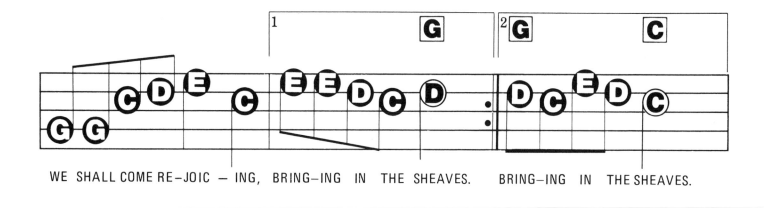

WE SHALL COME RE–JOIC — ING, BRING—ING IN THE SHEAVES. BRING—ING IN THE SHEAVES.

2.) SOWING IN THE SUNSHINE, SOWING IN THE SHADOWS,
FEARING NEITHER CLOUDS NOR WINTER'S CHILLING BREEZE;
BY AND BY THE HARVEST, AND THE LABOR ENDED,
WE SHALL COME REJOICING,
BRINGING IN THE SHEAVES.
Chorus

3.) GOING FORTH WITH WEEPING, SOWING FOR THE MASTER,
THO' THE LOSS SUSTAINED OUR SPIRIT OFTEN GRIEVES;
WHEN OUR WEEPING'S OVER, HE WILL BID US WELCOME,
WE SHALL COME REJOICING,
BRINGING IN THE SHEAVES.
Chorus

Come Thou Almighty King

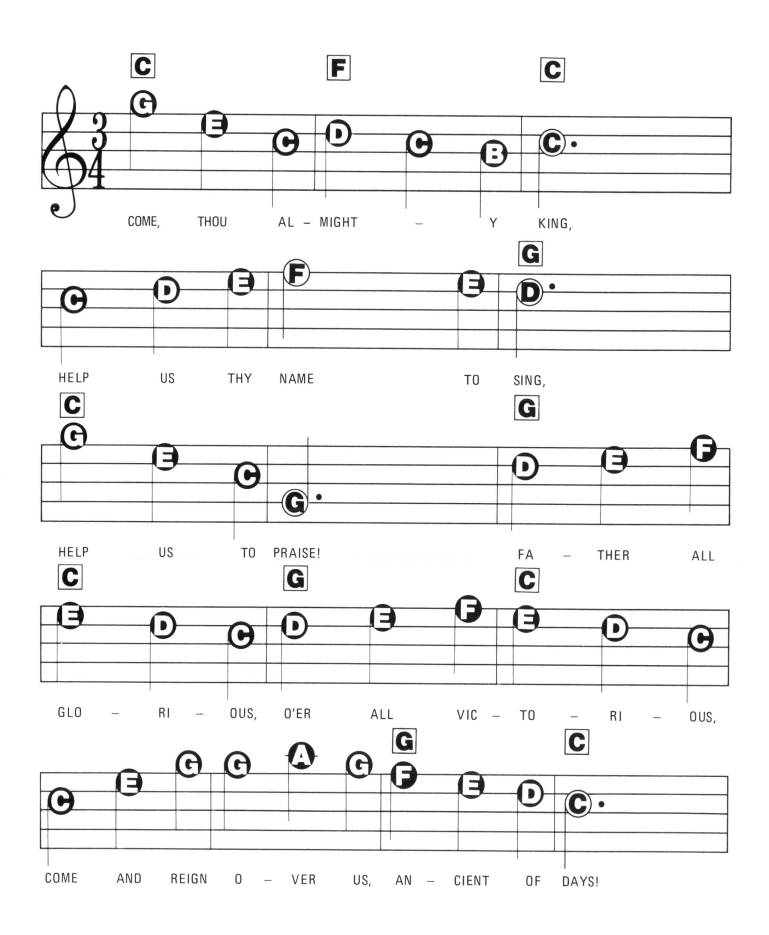

Doxology (Praise God From Whom All Blessings Flow)

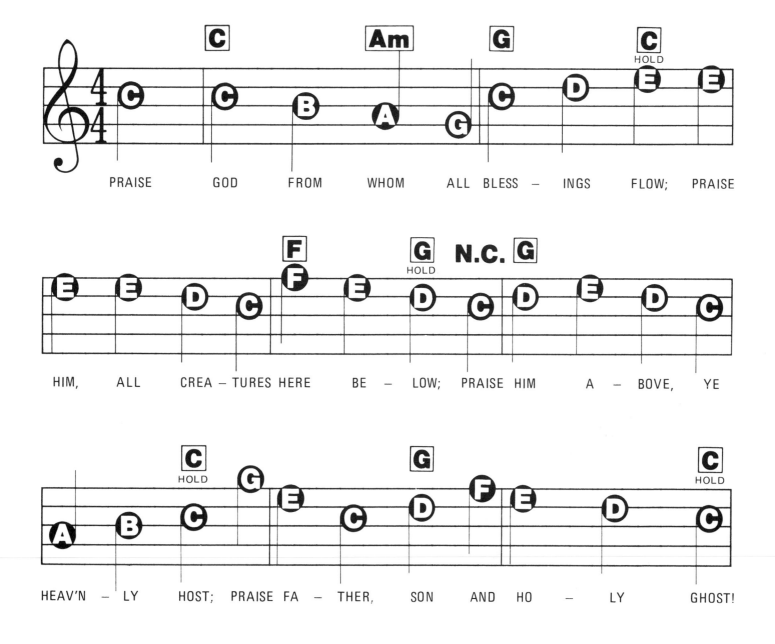

God Of Our Fathers Whose Almighty Hand

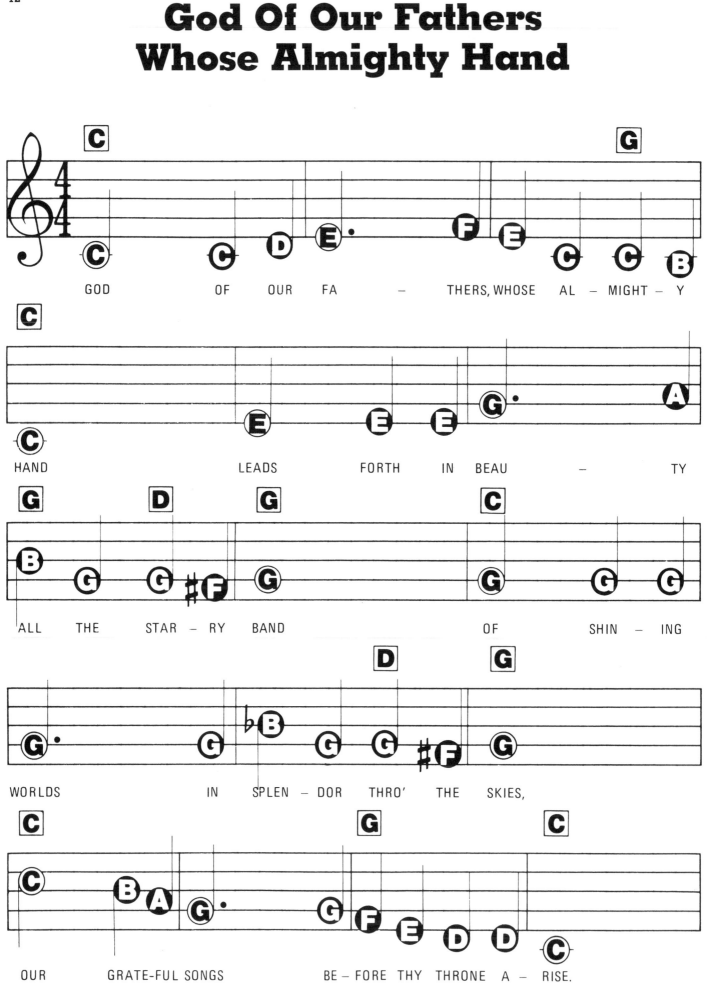

He's Got The Whole World In His Hands

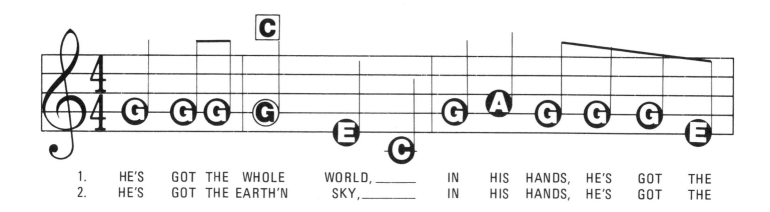

1. HE'S GOT THE WHOLE WORLD,_____ IN HIS HANDS, HE'S GOT THE
2. HE'S GOT THE EARTH'N SKY,_____ IN HIS HANDS, HE'S GOT THE

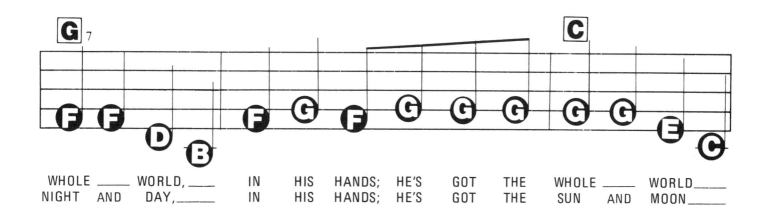

WHOLE ____ WORLD,____ IN HIS HANDS; HE'S GOT THE WHOLE ____ WORLD____
NIGHT AND DAY,____ IN HIS HANDS; HE'S GOT THE SUN AND MOON____

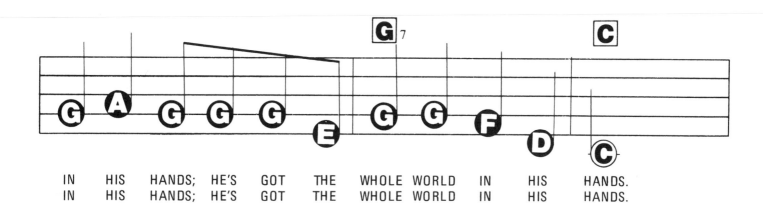

IN HIS HANDS; HE'S GOT THE WHOLE WORLD IN HIS HANDS.
IN HIS HANDS; HE'S GOT THE WHOLE WORLD IN HIS HANDS.

Holy God, We Praise Thy Name

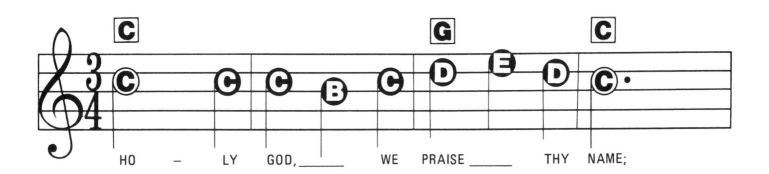

HO — LY GOD,_____ WE PRAISE _____ THY NAME;

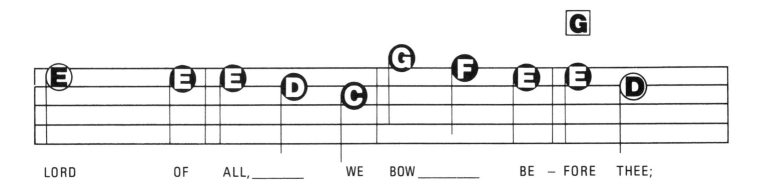

LORD OF ALL,_____ WE BOW _____ BE — FORE THEE;

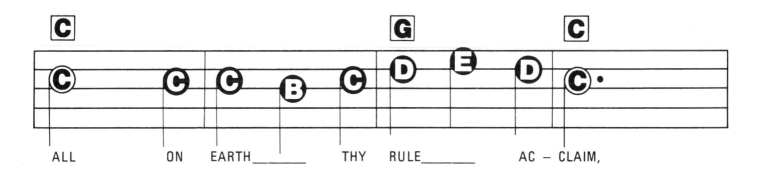

ALL ON EARTH_____ THY RULE_____ AC — CLAIM,

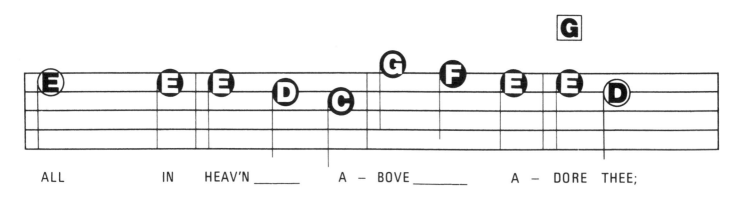

ALL IN HEAV'N_____ A — BOVE_____ A — DORE THEE;

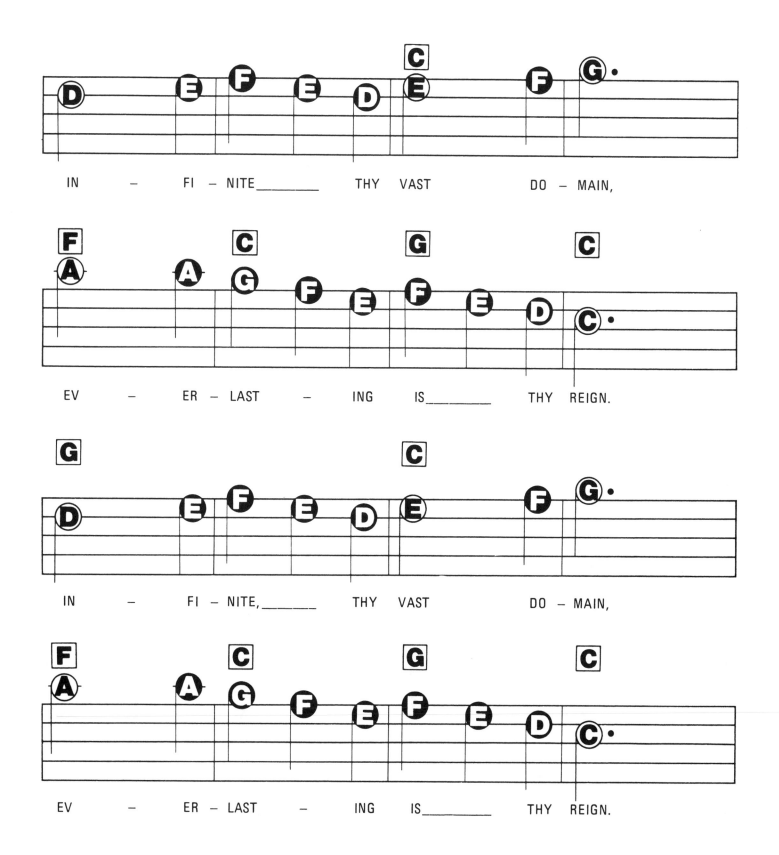

2.) HARK! THE LOUD CELESTIAL HYMN
ANGEL CHOIRS ABOVE ARE RAISING;
CHERUBIM AND SERAPHIM
IN UNCEASING CHORUS PRAISING;
FILL THE HEAV'NS WITH SWEET ACCORD;
HOLY, HOLY, HOLY, LORD!
FILL THE HEAV'NS WITH SWEET ACCORD;
HOLY, HOLY, HOLY, LORD!

3.) HOLY FATHER, HOLY SON,
HOLY SPIRIT, THREE WE NAME THEE;
WHILE IN ESSENCE ONLY ONE,
UNDIVIDED GOD WE CLAIM THEE;
AND ADORING, BEND THE KNEE,
WHILE WE OWN THE MYSTERY.
AND ADORING, BEND THE KNEE,
WHILE WE OWN THE MYSTERY.

Holy, Holy, Holy

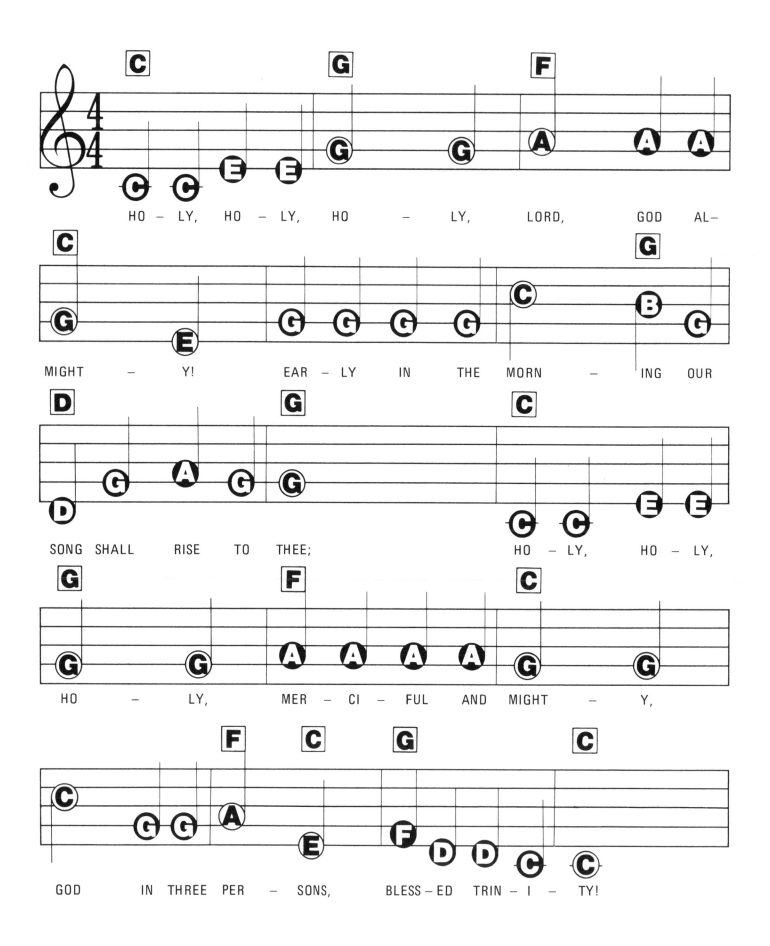

In The Sweet By And By

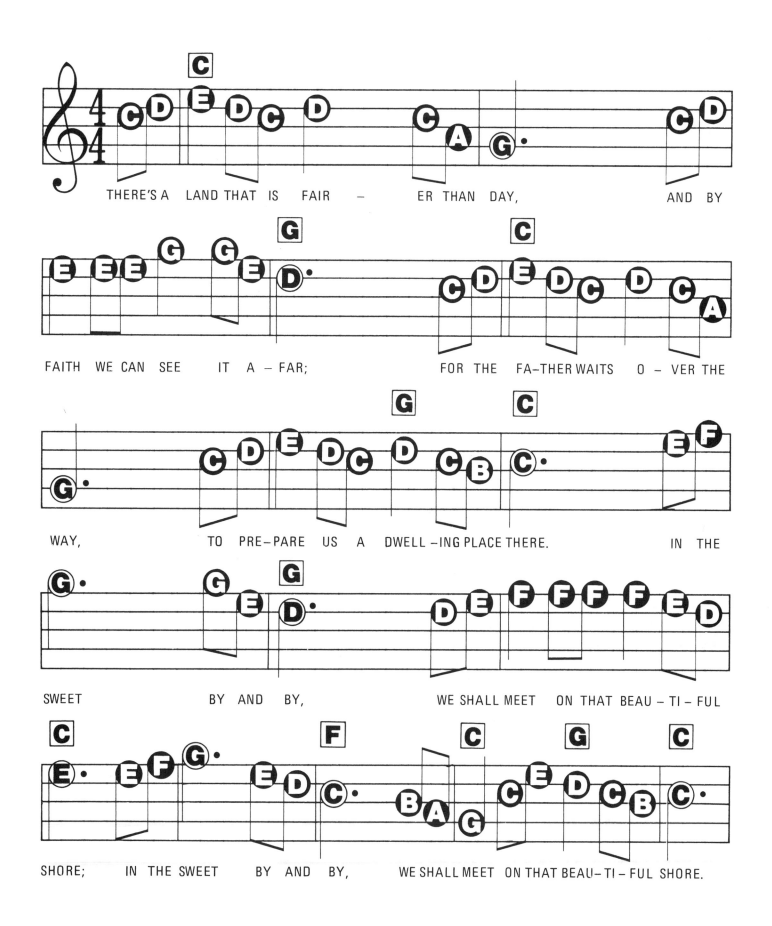

Joshua Fit De Battle Of Jericho

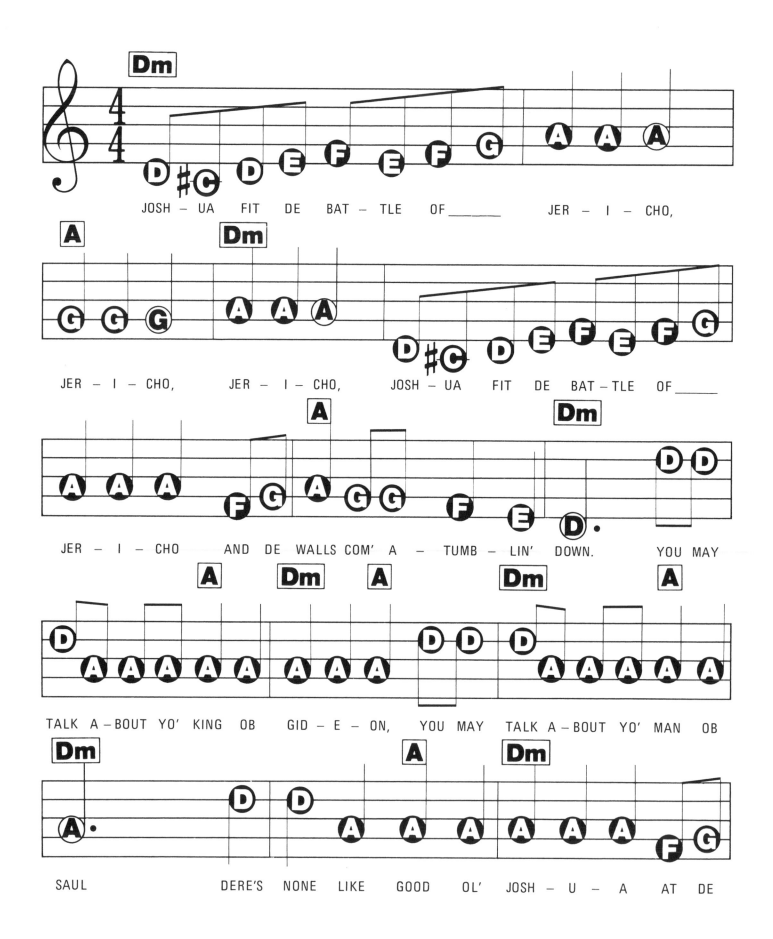

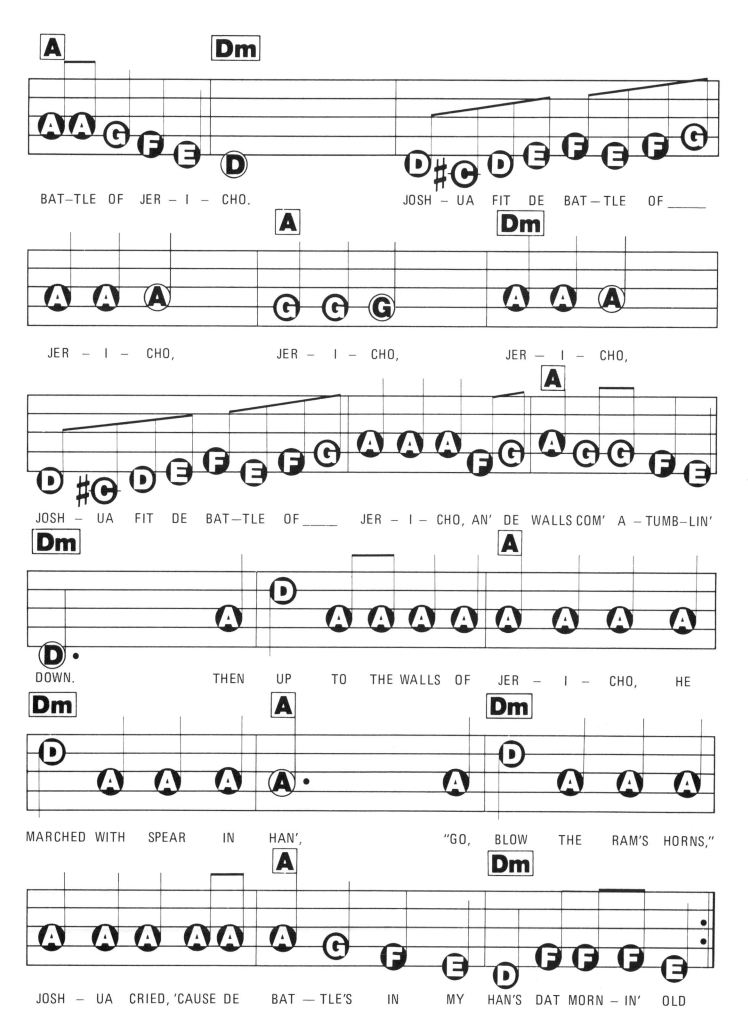

Jesus Christ Is Risen Today

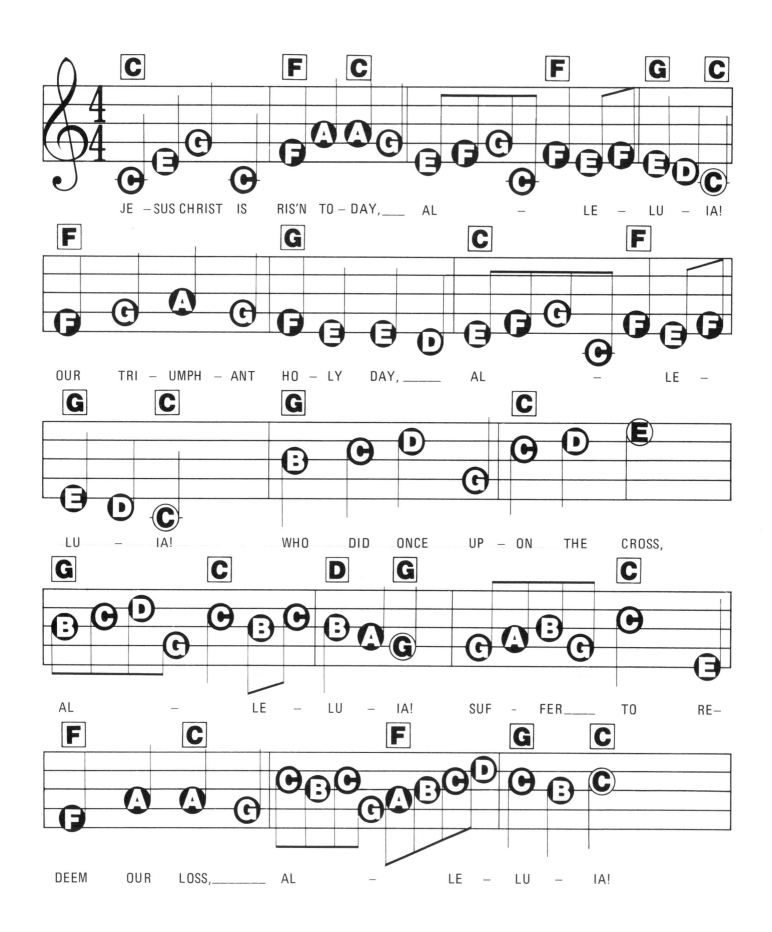

Kumbaya

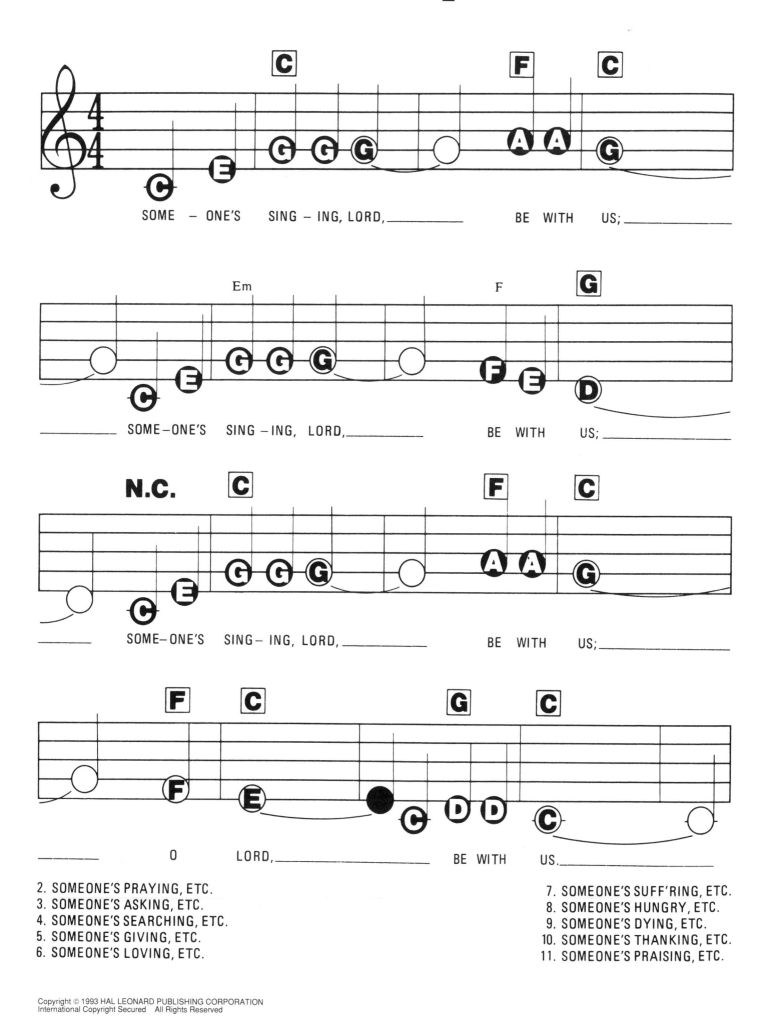

2. SOMEONE'S PRAYING, ETC.
3. SOMEONE'S ASKING, ETC.
4. SOMEONE'S SEARCHING, ETC.
5. SOMEONE'S GIVING, ETC.
6. SOMEONE'S LOVING, ETC.

7. SOMEONE'S SUFF'RING, ETC.
8. SOMEONE'S HUNGRY, ETC.
9. SOMEONE'S DYING, ETC.
10. SOMEONE'S THANKING, ETC.
11. SOMEONE'S PRAISING, ETC.

Little Brown Church In The Vale

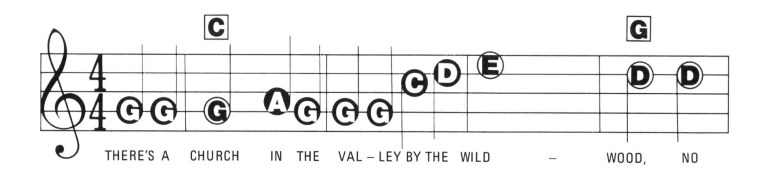

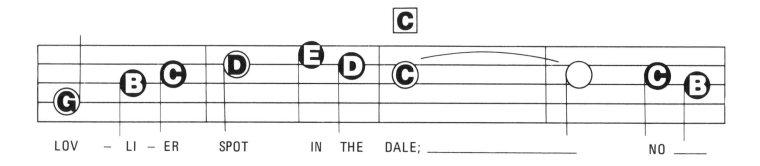

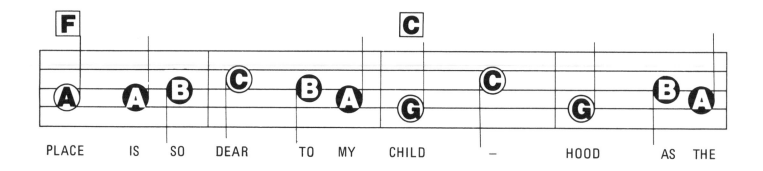

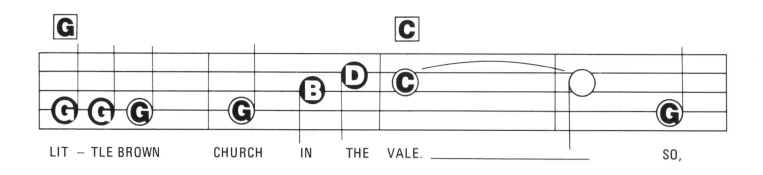

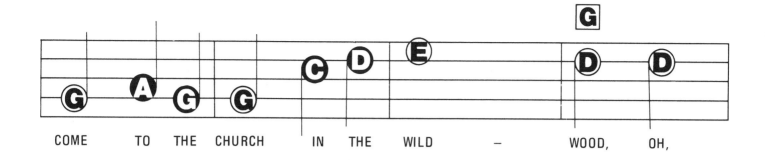

COME   TO   THE   CHURCH   IN   THE   WILD   —   WOOD,   OH,

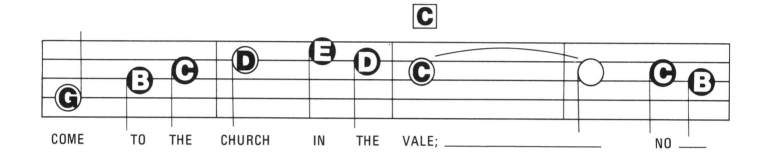

COME   TO   THE   CHURCH   IN   THE   VALE; _____   NO ___

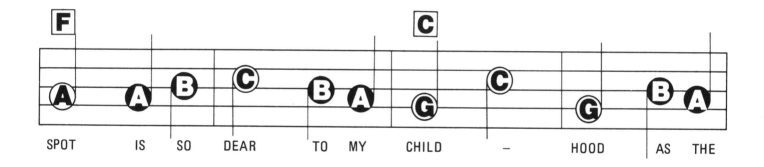

SPOT   IS   SO   DEAR   TO   MY   CHILD   —   HOOD   AS   THE

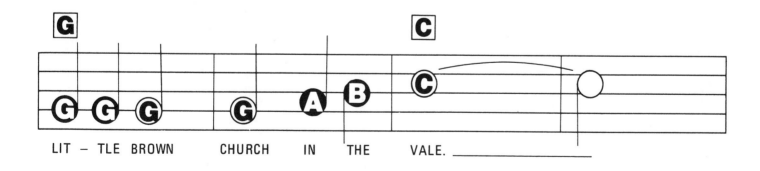

LIT – TLE BROWN   CHURCH   IN   THE   VALE. _____

A Mighty Fortress Is Our God

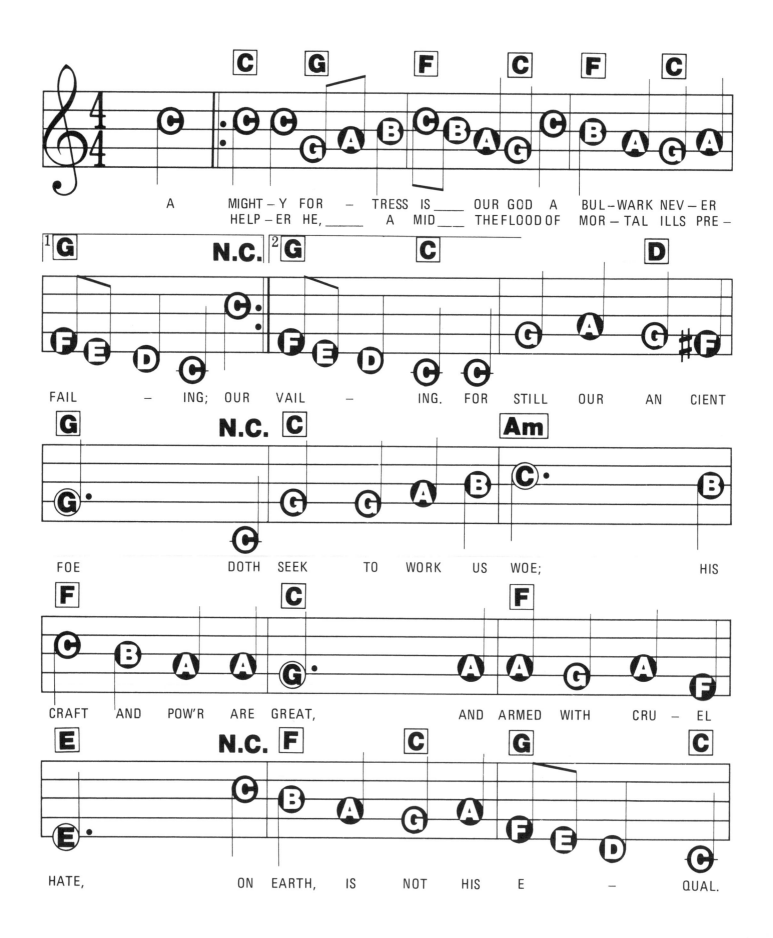

My Faith Looks Up To Thee

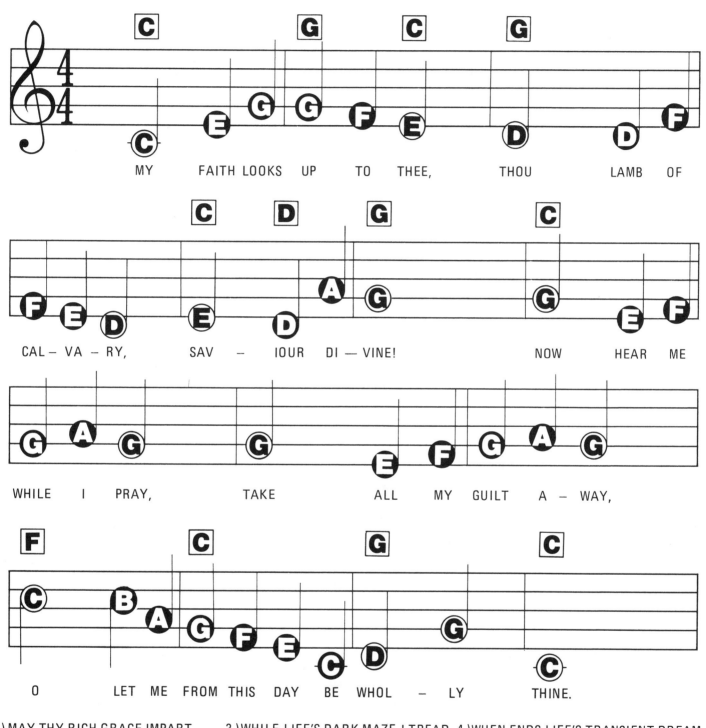

2.) MAY THY RICH GRACE IMPART
STRENGTH TO MY FAINTING HEART,
MY ZEAL INSPIRE;
AS THOU HAST DIED FOR ME,
O MAY MY LOVE TO THEE
PURE, WARM AND CHANGELESS BE,
A LIVING FIRE!

3.) WHILE LIFE'S DARK MAZE I TREAD,
AND GRIEFS AROUND ME SPREAD,
BE THOU MY GUIDE;
BID DARKNESS TURN TO DAY,
WIPE SORROW'S TEARS AWAY,
NOR LET ME EVER STRAY
FROM THEE ASIDE.

4.) WHEN ENDS LIFE'S TRANSIENT DREAM,
WHEN DEATH'S COLD, SULLEN STREAM
SHALL O'ER ME ROLL;
BLEST SAVIOR, THEN, IN LOVE,
FEAR AND DISTRUST REMOVE;
O BEAR ME SAFE ABOVE,
A RANSOMED SOUL!

Nearer, My God, To Thee

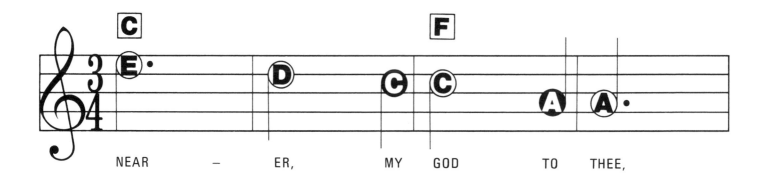

NEAR — ER, MY GOD TO THEE,

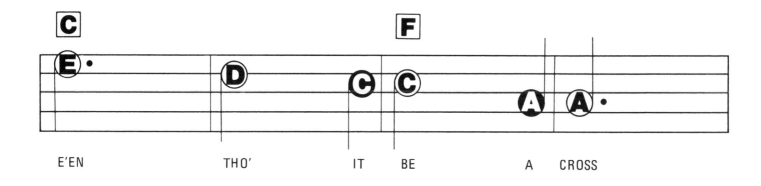

NEAR — ER TO THEE!_____

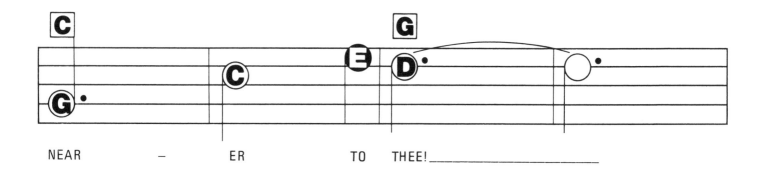

E'EN THO' IT BE A CROSS

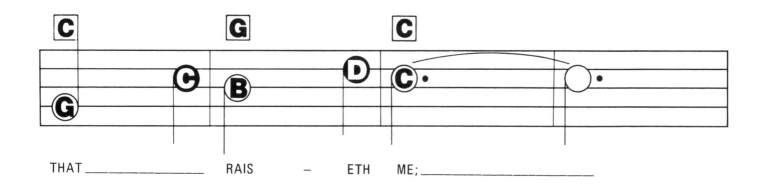

THAT_____ RAIS — ETH ME;_____

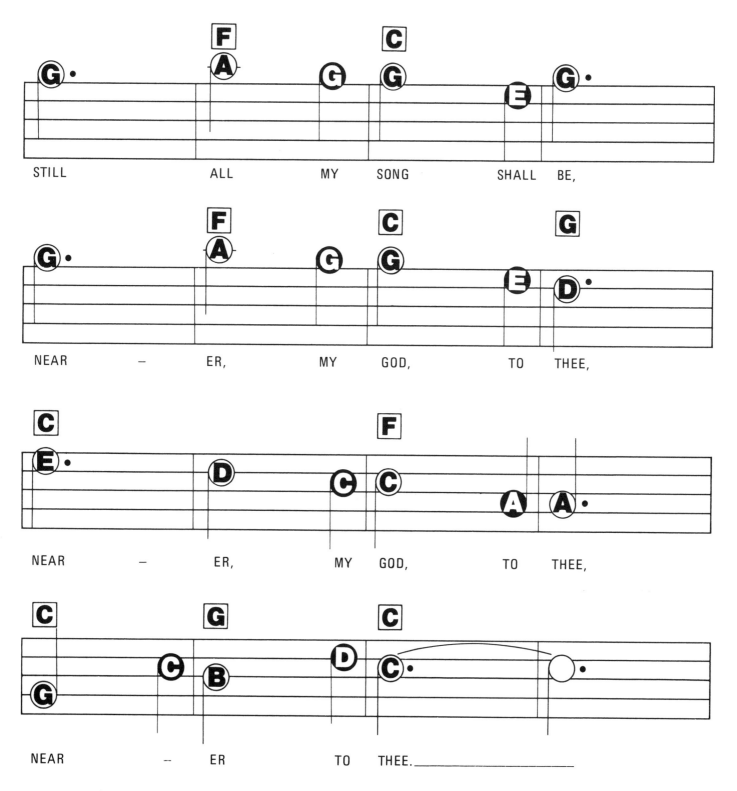

STILL   ALL   MY   SONG   SHALL   BE,

NEAR   —   ER,   MY   GOD,   TO   THEE,

NEAR   —   ER,   MY   GOD,   TO   THEE,

NEAR   —   ER   TO   THEE._____

2. THO' LIKE THE WANDERER,
   THE SUN GONE DOWN,
   DARKNESS BE OVER ME,
   MY REST A STONE,
   YET IN MY DREAMS I'D BE,
   NEARER, MY GOD, TO THEE,
   NEARER, MY GOD, TO THEE,
   NEARER TO THEE.

3. THERE LET THE WAY APPEAR
   STEPS UNTO HEAV'N;
   ALL THAT THOU SENDEST ME
   IN MERCY GIV'N;
   ANGELS TO BECKON ME,
   NEARER, MY GOD, TO THEE,
   NEARER, MY GOD, TO THEE,
   NEARER TO THEE.

4. OR IF ON JOYFUL WING
   CLEAVING THE SKY,
   SUN, MOON, AND STARS FORGOT,
   UPWARD I FLY,
   STILL ALL MY SONG SHALL BE,
   NEARER, MY GOD, TO THEE,
   NEARER, MY GOD, TO THEE,
   NEARER TO THEE.

Nobody Knows
The Trouble I've Seen

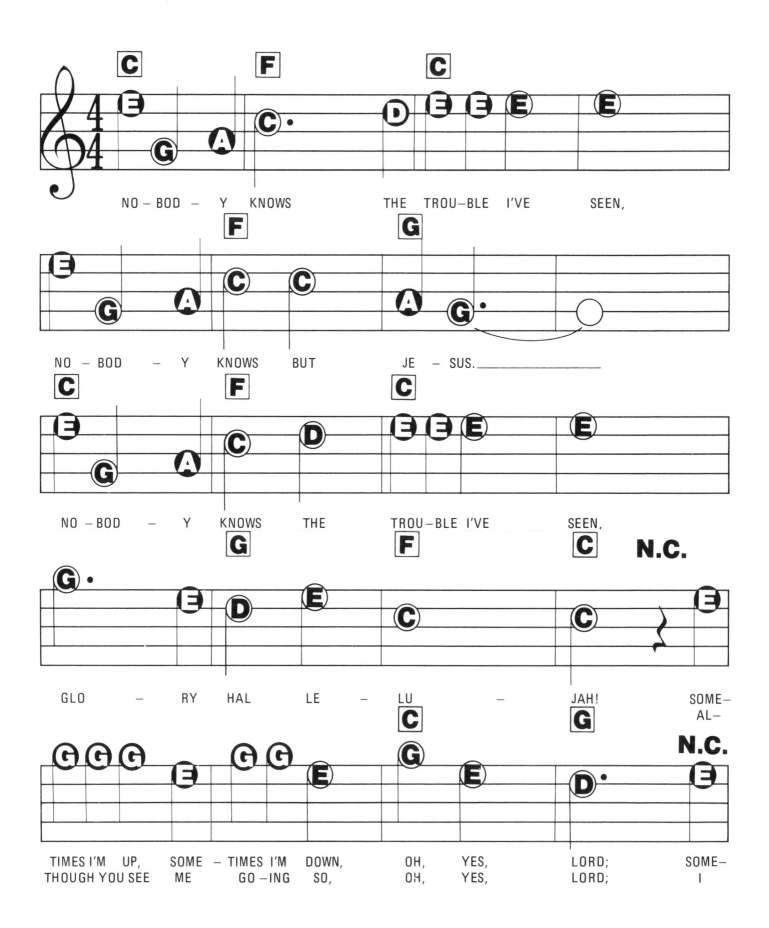

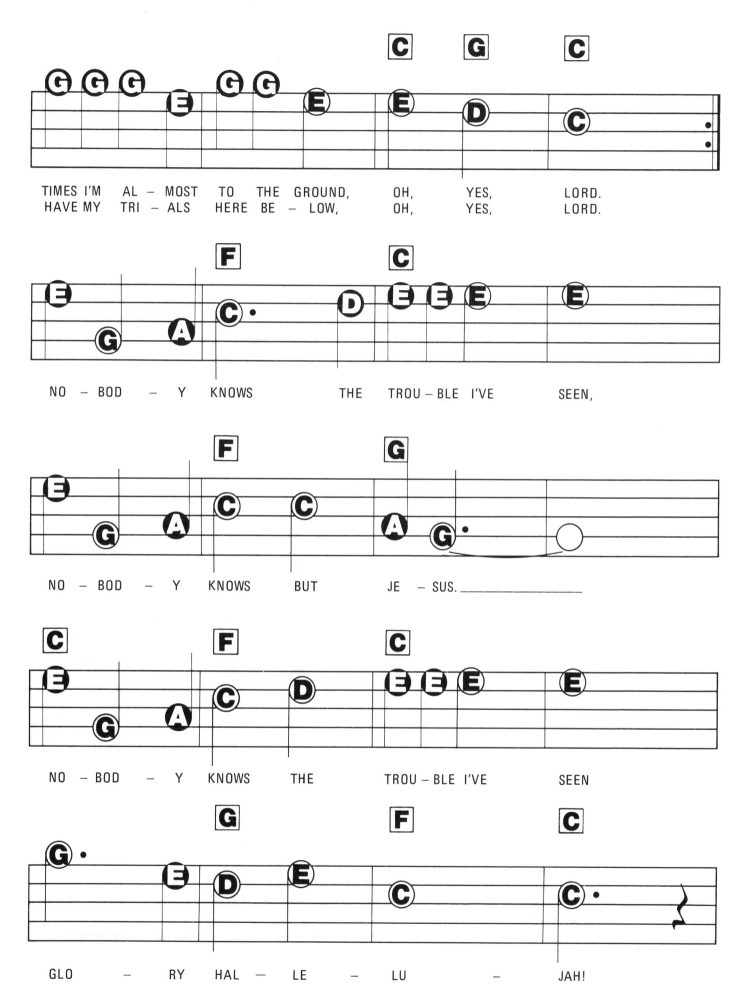

Now Thank We All Our God

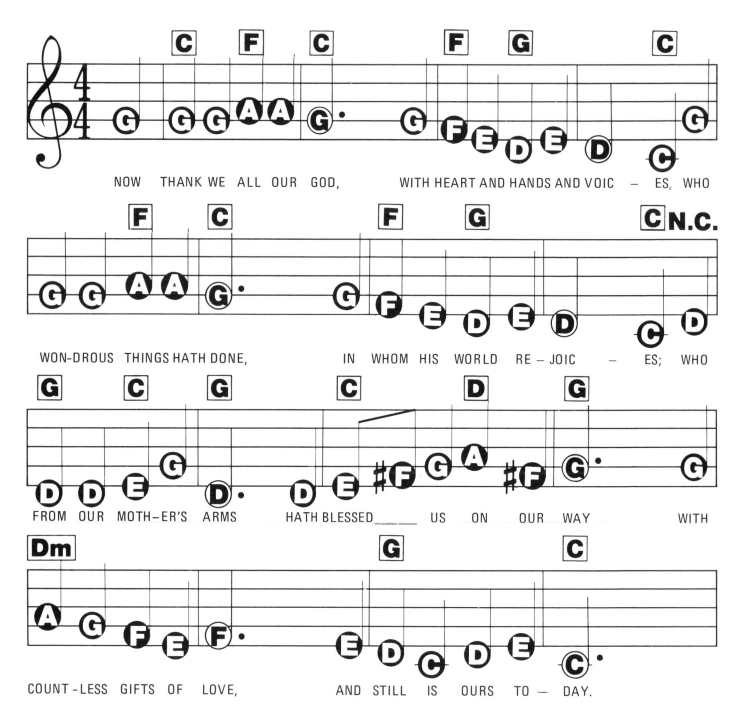

2.) O MAY THIS BOUNTEOUS GOD,
THROUGH ALL OUR LIFE BE NEAR US!
WITH EVER JOYFUL HEARTS
AND BLESSED PEACE TO CHEER US;
AND KEEP US IN HIS GRACE,
AND GUIDE US WHEN PERPLEXED,
AND FREE US FROM ALL ILLS
IN THIS WORLD AND THE NEXT.

3.) ALL PRAISE AND THANKS TO GOD,
THE FATHER NOW BE GIVEN,
THE SON AND SPIRIT BLESSED
WHO REIGN IN HIGHEST HEAVEN;
ETERNAL, TRIUNE GOD,
WHOM EARTH AND HEAV'N ADORE;
FOR THUS IT WAS, IS NOW,
AND SHALL BE EVERMORE.

Praise To The Lord

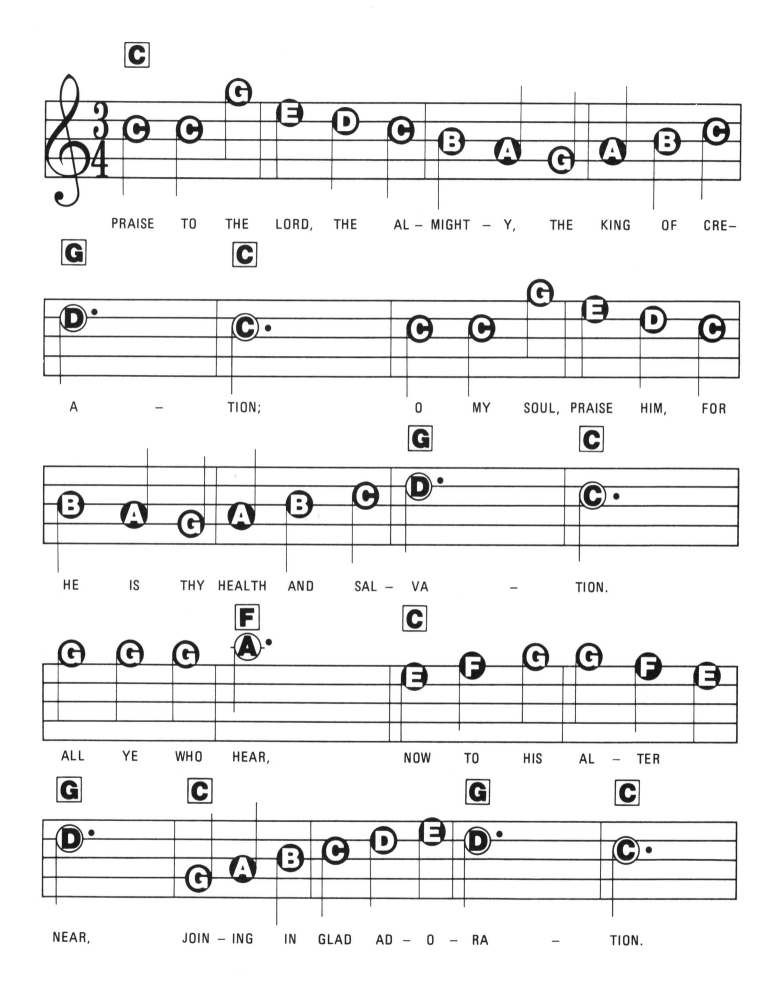

Sweet Hour Of Prayer

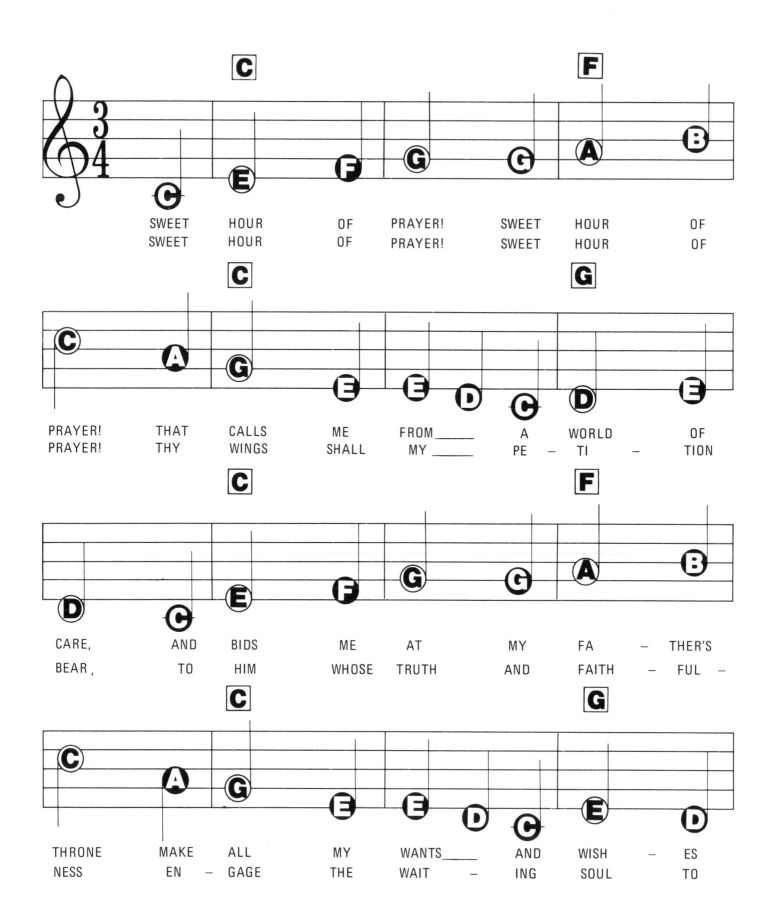

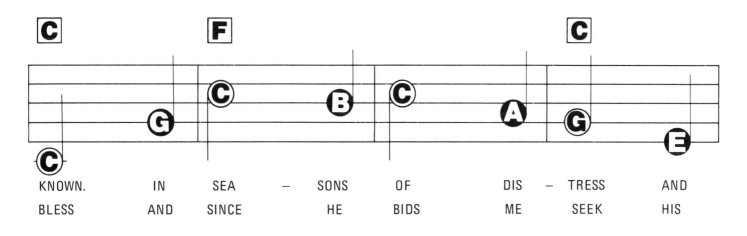

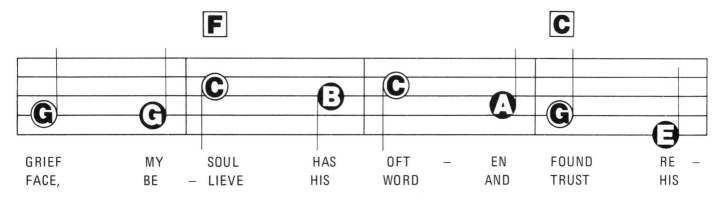

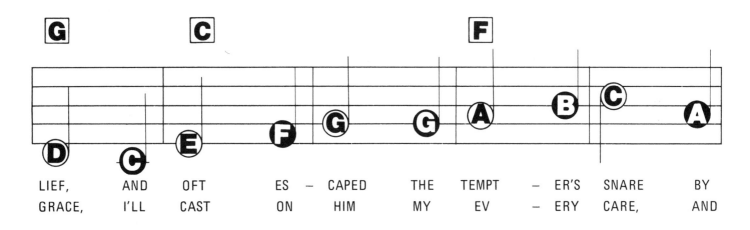

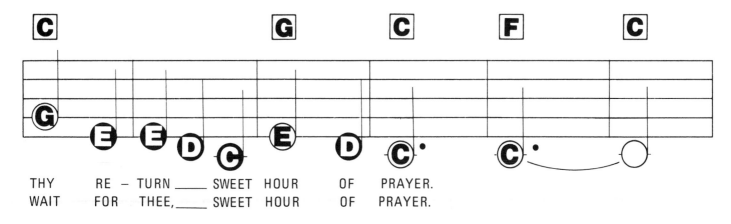

Rock Of Ages

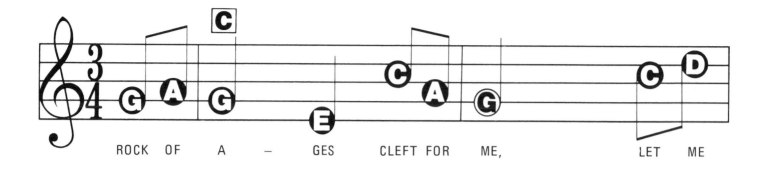

ROCK OF A — GES   CLEFT FOR   ME,   LET   ME

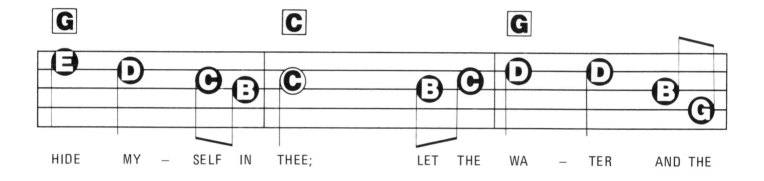

HIDE   MY — SELF   IN   THEE;   LET THE   WA — TER   AND THE

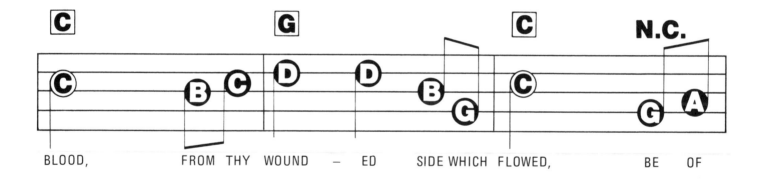

BLOOD,   FROM THY WOUND — ED   SIDE WHICH FLOWED,   BE   OF

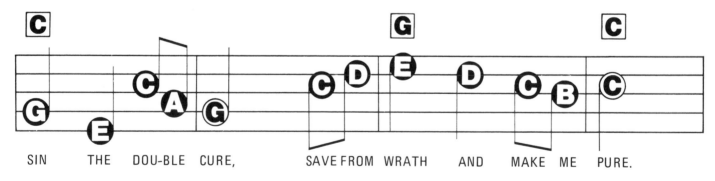

SIN   THE   DOU-BLE   CURE,   SAVE FROM WRATH   AND   MAKE ME   PURE.

2.) COULD MY TEARS FOREVER FLOW,
COULD MY ZEAL NO LANGUOR KNOW,
THESE FOR SIN COULD NOT ATONE;
THOU MUST SAVE, AND THOU ALONE:
IN MY HAND NO PRICE I BRING,
SIMPLY TO THY CROSS I CLING.

3.) WHILE I DRAW THIS FLEETING BREATH,
WHEN MY EYES SHALL CLOSE IN DEATH,
WHEN I RISE TO WORLDS UNKNOWN,
AND BEHOLD THEE ON THY THRONE
ROCK OF AGES, CLEFT FOR ME,
LET ME HIDE MYSELF IN THEE.

Swing Low, Sweet Chariot

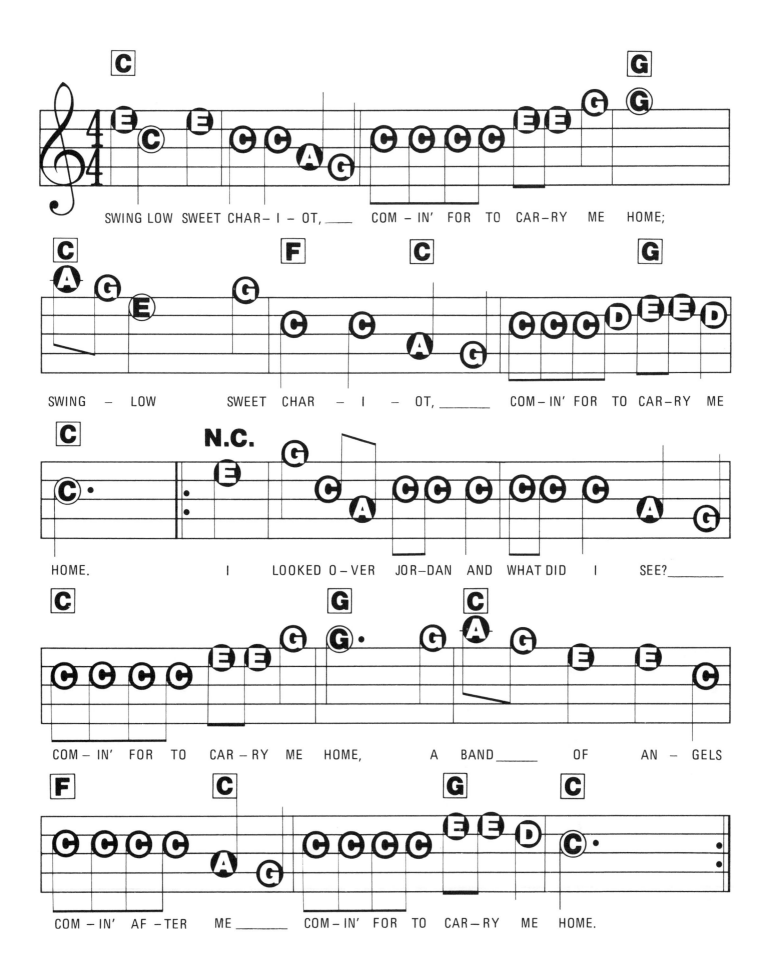

What A Friend We Have In Jesus

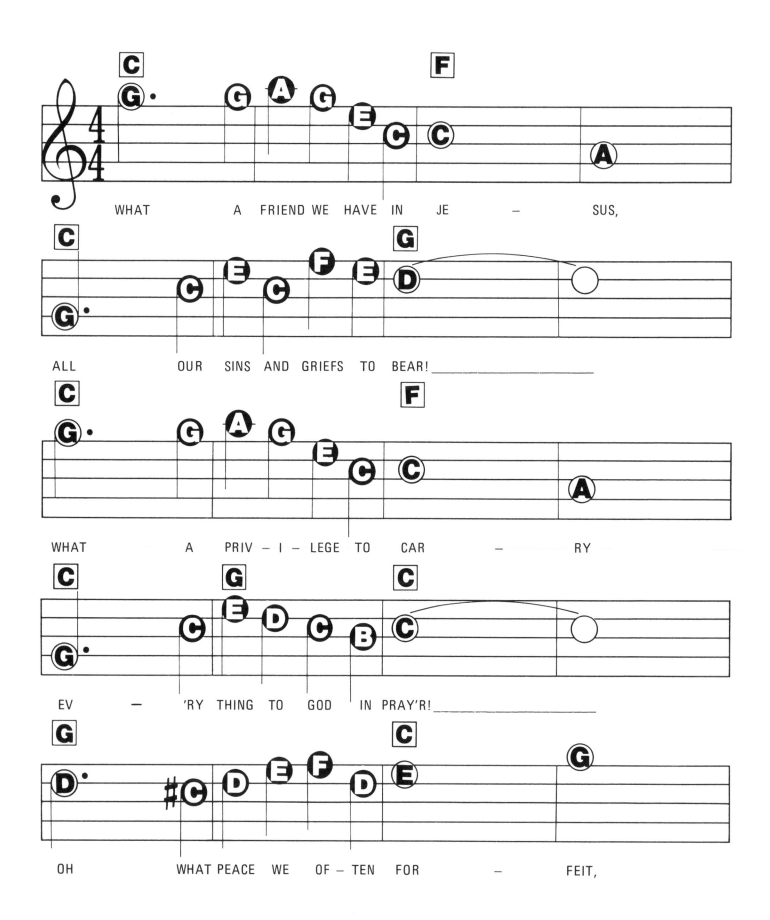

WHAT A FRIEND WE HAVE IN JE — SUS,

ALL OUR SINS AND GRIEFS TO BEAR! _____

WHAT A PRIV — I — LEGE TO CAR — RY

EV — 'RY THING TO GOD IN PRAY'R! _____

OH WHAT PEACE WE OF — TEN FOR — FEIT,

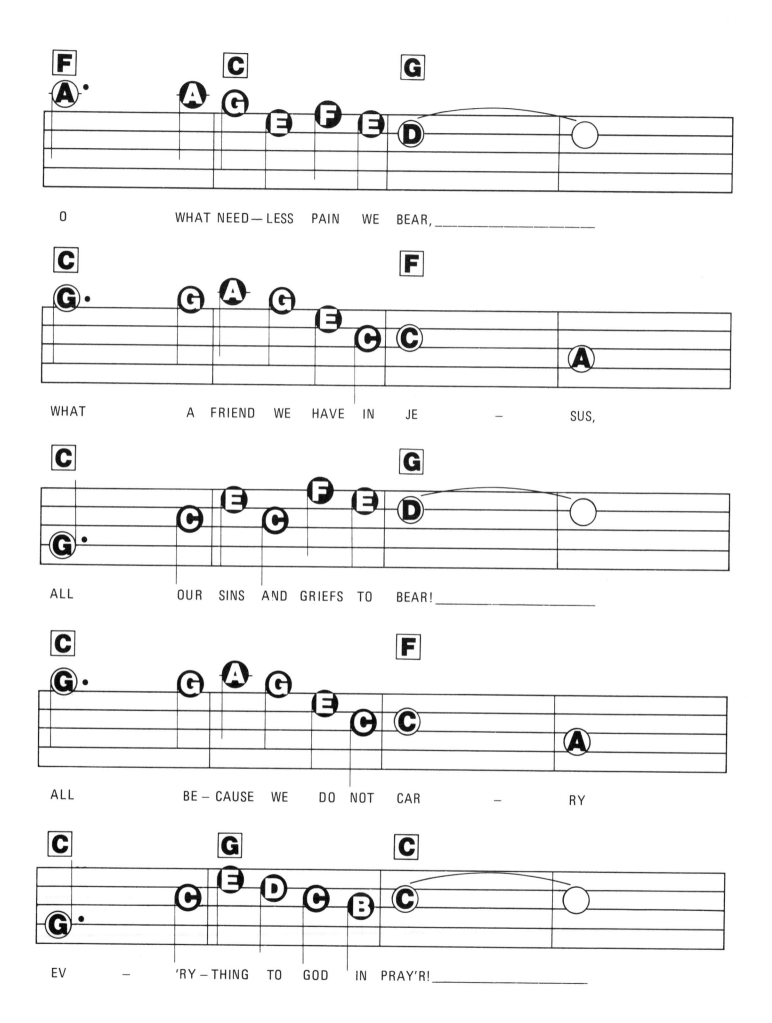

Whispering Hope

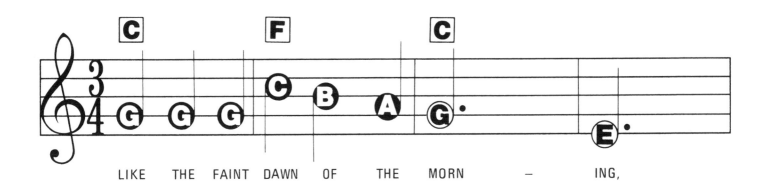

LIKE   THE   FAINT   DAWN   OF   THE   MORN   —   ING,

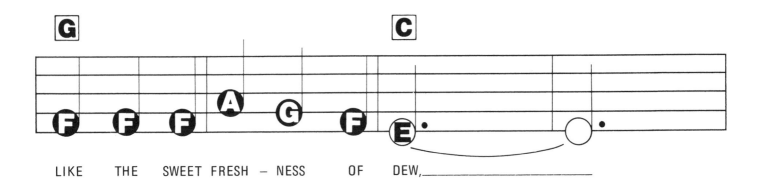

LIKE   THE   SWEET   FRESH — NESS   OF   DEW,_____

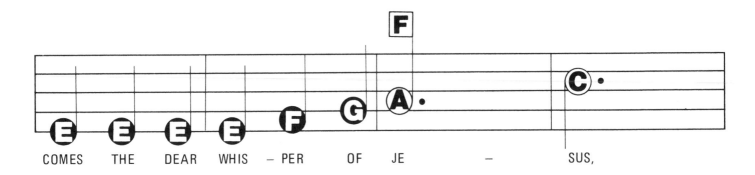

COMES   THE   DEAR   WHIS — PER   OF   JE   —   SUS,

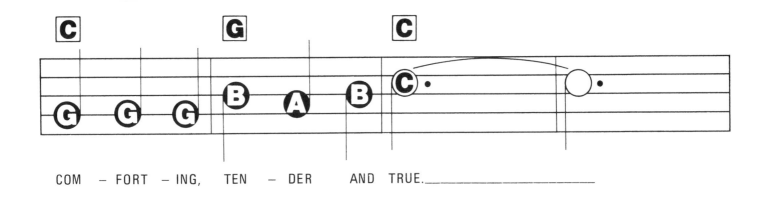

COM — FORT — ING,   TEN — DER   AND   TRUE._____

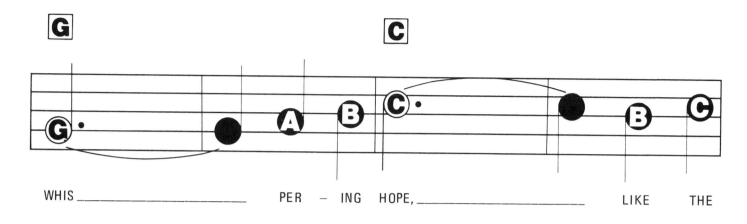

WHIS_____ PER – ING HOPE,_____ LIKE THE

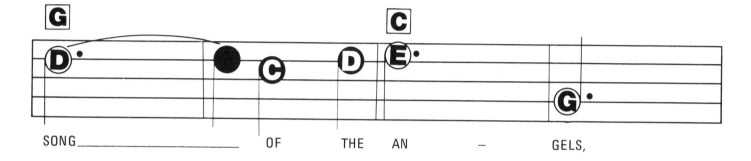

SONG_____ OF THE AN — GELS,

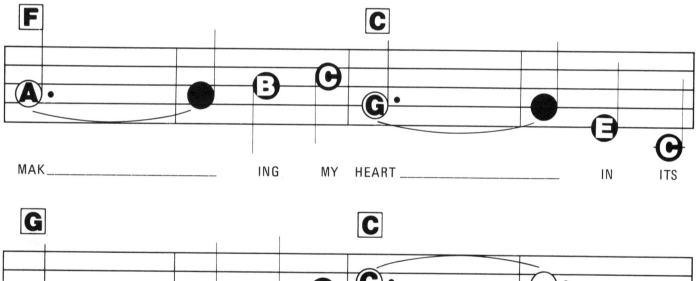

MAK_____ ING MY HEART_____ IN ITS

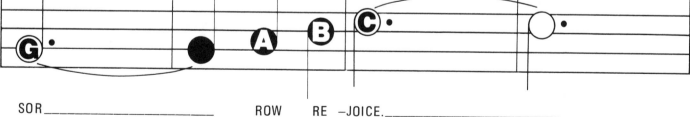

SOR_____ ROW RE –JOICE._____

2. SINGING THE SONG OF FORGIVENESS,
   SOFTLY I HEAR IN MY SOUL,
   JESUS HAS CONQUERED FOREVER
   SIN WITH ITS FEARFUL CONTROL

3. HOPE IS AN ANCHOR TO KEEP US,
   HOLDING BOTH STEADFAST AND SURE:
   HOPE BRINGS A WONDERFUL CLEANSING,
   THRO' HIS BLOOD, MAKING US PURE.

Were You There?

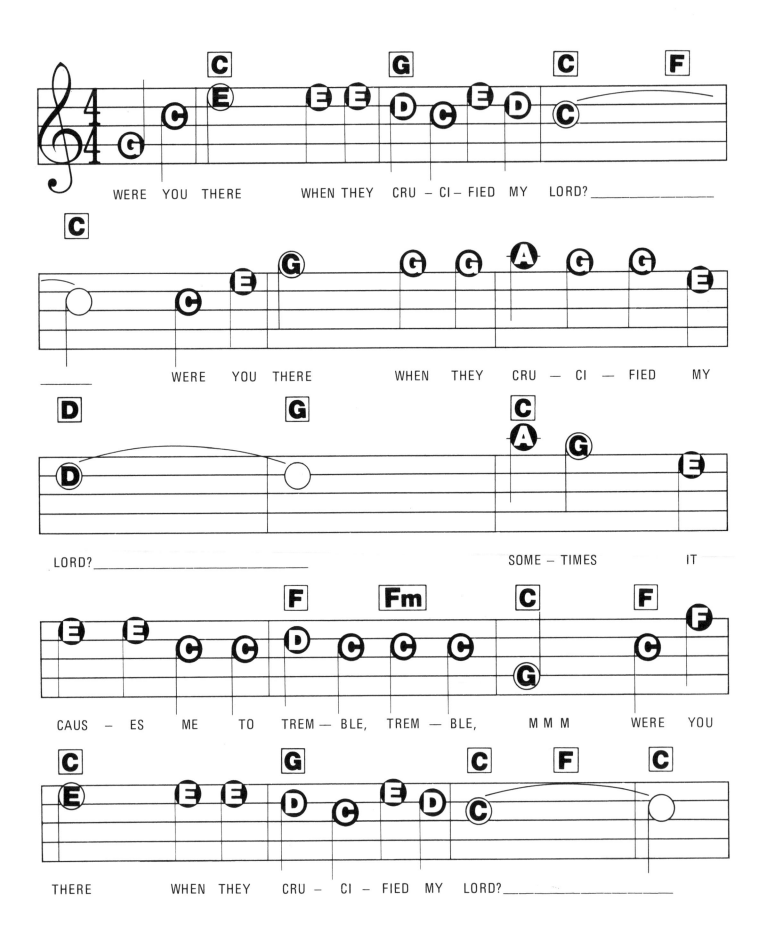